THE ULTIMATE ACTIVITY BOOK FOR MAD SCIENTISTS

THE ULTIMATE ACTIVITY BOOK FOR MAD SCIENTISTS

JOE RHATIGAN   ILLUSTRATIONS BY ANTHONY OWSLEY

MoonDance

Brimming with creative inspiration, how-to projects, and useful information to enrich your everyday life, Quarto Knows is a favorite destination for those pursuing their interests and passions. Visit our site and dig deeper with our books into your area of interest: Quarto Creates, Quarto Cooks, Quarto Homes, Quarto Lives, Quarto Drives, Quarto Explores, Quarto Gifts, or Quarto Kids.

© 2017 Quarto Publishing Group USA Inc.
Text © 2017 Joe Rhatigan

First published in 2017 by MoonDance Press, an imprint of The Quarto Group.
26391 Crown Valley Parkway, Suite 220, Mission Viejo, CA 92691, USA.
T (949) 380-7510 **F** (949) 380-7575 **www.QuartoKnows.com**

MoonDance Press titles are also available at discount for retail, wholesale, promotional, and bulk purchase. For details, contact the Special Sales Manager by email at specialsales@quarto.com or by mail at The Quarto Group, Attn: Special Sales Manager, 100 Cummings Center, Suite 265D, Beverly, MA 01915, USA.

ISBN: 978-1-63322-163-5

Design & page layout: Melissa Gerber

Printed in China
10 9 8 7 6 5 4

ARE YOU A SCIENTIST?

WARNING

This book is for scientists only! Worried you're not a scientist? Take this short quiz to find out.

Do you have a white lab coat?
Yes or No

Do you have crazy Albert Einstein hair?
Yes or No

Do you yell "Eureka!" any time you come up with a great idea?
Yes or No

Do you have a faithful assistant?
Yes or No

Do you plan on doing all the activities in this book?
Yes or No

It doesn't matter if you answered "yes" or "no" to any of these questions! This was just a fun little quiz to get you ready for all the big fun inside this book. Quizzes, doodles, puzzles, and more await you and your curious scientific mind. So grab a pencil, mess up your hair a little bit for that mad scientist look, and have fun!

PERIODIC TABLE OF THE ELEMENTS WORD SEARCH

Elements are substances in the universe that are made up of only one kind of atom, meaning they can't be broken apart into other substances. On the opposite page is the periodic table of elements, a chart that includes the abbreviations for all of the elements. If you ever space out in science class, you might notice that some of the abbreviations can be put together to form words. Create as many words and sentences as you can using only element abbreviations (no turning them backward).

_____
_____
_____
_____
_____
_____
_____
_____
_____
_____
_____
_____
_____
_____
_____

PERIODIC TABLE OF THE ELEMENTS

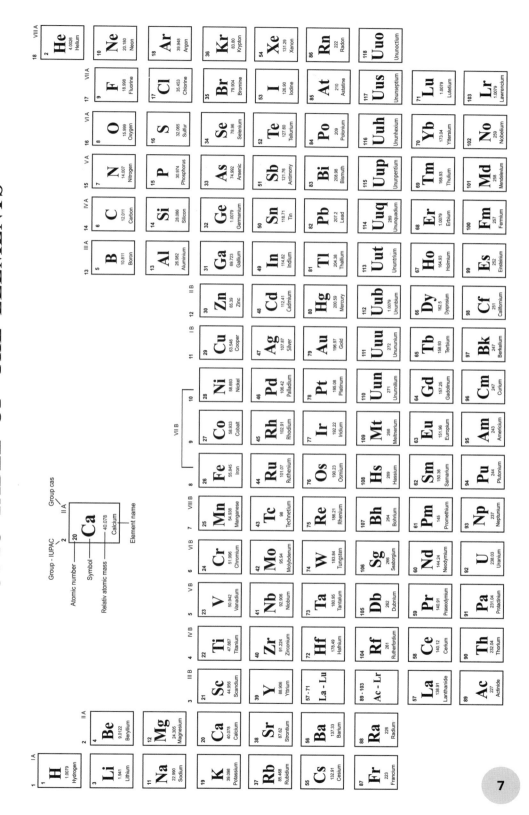

IDENTIFY THESE NEW SPECIES

Most of the animals we know about (like cats and elephants) have already been discovered. But in 2015, scientists discovered a frog that can change its texture, a hog-nosed rat, and a ninja lanternshark. Now it's your turn. Identify some of the new species in the forest on pages 10 and 11. Give them a scientific name, a common name, and tell us a cool fact about them.

Interesting Fact: When scientists discover a new species of plant, animal, or insect they give it a scientific name, which means a name in Latin that other scientists can use to identify it. The first person to do this was a man named Carl von Linné who liked Latin so much he changed his name to Carolus Linnaeus. He invented *binomial nomenclature*, a fancy term for naming species.

Scientific name:

_____

Common name:

_____

Cool facts:

_____
_____
_____

Scientific name:

_____

Common name:

_____

Cool facts:

_____
_____
_____

Scientific name:

_____

Common name:

_____

Cool facts:

_____
_____
_____

Scientific name:

_____

Common name:

_____

Cool facts:

_____
_____
_____

Scientific name:

_____

Common name:

_____

Cool facts:

_____
_____
_____

Scientific name:

_____

Common name:

_____

Cool facts:

_____
_____
_____

Scientific name:

_____

Common name:

_____

Cool facts:

_____
_____
_____

BLACK HOLE

When huge stars die, they collapse in on themselves and form black holes, areas that nothing can escape getting sucked into. Even light gets pulled into black holes. So do lamps, shoes, and dinosaurs—if they end up in space. Draw some things getting sucked toward this black hole.

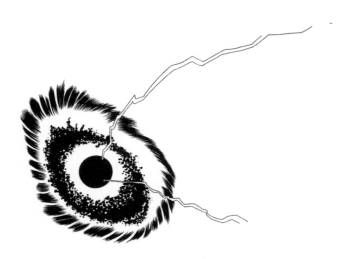

ANIMAL COUSINS

In 1859, a scientist named Charles Darwin came up with the Theory of Evolution. After years of research, he figured out that species change over time to become new species. When the environment where a species lives changes, some members of the species are different from the other ones and are better at surviving in the new environment. After many, many years and many, many changes, they become a new species. Even humans came from ancient species of apes that began to walk on two legs and developed language and culture over millions of years. Some animals alive today are very different, but they evolved from the same ancestor. Guess which two species in each group are most closely related. **Answers on page 143.**

1.

Dinosaur

Bat

Bird

2.

Whale

Fish

Rhino

3.

Humans

Lemurs

Bears

4.

Koala

Kangaroo

Raccoon

5.

Ladybug

Fish

Crab

6.

Sunflower

Seaweed

Mushroom

7.
Turtle
Snake
Alligator

8.
Camel
Horse
Hippo

9.
Octopus
Snail
Jellyfish

10.
Rabbit
Hedgehog
Mole

SCRAMBLED SCIENTISTS

There are all kinds of different jobs for people who are interested in science. Unscramble the words below to find out what some of them are. Use the upside-down hints if you need help. **Answers on page 143.**

1. Hapiarmtsc

_____

Hint: These healthcare professionals use chemistry to help people use medicine safely.

2. Logsobiit

_____

Hint: Scientists with this job study life on earth, including plants and animals.

3. Rorssfoep

_____

Hint: These folks teach all kinds of science at colleges and universities.

4. Nengriee

_____

Hint: These handy people use math and science to design machines and other difficult things.

5. Ityschpsi

_____

Hint: With a lot of help from math and Isaac Newton, these scientists study matter and energy.

6. Crspitaitsyh

_____

Hint: For people suffering from mental illnesses, this type of psychologist can help with medication and treatment.

7. Moosegreloitt

_____

Hint: You might see some of these people on TV — they study and predict the weather.

8. Ivnrtosnaeemlint

_____

Hint: These awesome activists study the natural world and fight to protect it from climate change and human destruction.

9. Oeogsiglt

_____

Hint: They study rocks, how the Earth is made, and how the planet changes over time.

10. Anotbtsi

_____

Hint: These scientists specialize in studying plants.

EUREKA!

When scientists make an important discovery, they get pretty excited. Sometimes they shout weird things, especially in movies. See what other words you can make out of these scientific exclamations. If you want to make a game out of it, grab a friend and some paper. Give yourselves a time limit and one of these exclamations. Once you're done coming up with as many words as possible, check your answers. Cross out any words you have in common. Whoever has the most unique words left over, wins.

Answers on page 143.

Eureka!

_____

_____

_____

_____

_____

_____

It's alive!

_____

_____

_____

_____

_____

What's that?

_____

_____

_____

_____

_____

Yikes!

_____

_____

_____

_____

Awesome!

_____

_____

_____

_____

What are you going to say when you make a giant discovery? How many words can you find in your exclamation?

IT'S ELEMENT-ARY

Did you know that everything in the universe is made up of tiny particles called atoms? There are different kinds of atoms that make up different elements, like you saw on the periodic table of the elements on page 7. Water is made up of two hydrogen atoms and one oxygen atom. On the next page is a grid of hydrogen and oxygen. Grab a friend, and see how much water you can make!

Rules: You and your friend take turns drawing lines to create water molecules. You can create one water molecule (two Hs and one O) with each turn using horizontal, diagonal, and vertical lines only. You can only use each atom once. Keep going until there are no more molecules left to make. Whoever makes the last one, wins!

Sample Game

The first water molecule has been found. How many more can you locate in this sample game?

H	O	H	O
O	O	H	H
H	O	O	O
H	H	O	O
O	H	O	H

O	O	H	H	H	O	H	O	O	H	O	H	O
H	O	H	H	O	H	O	H	O	O	H	O	O
O	H	O	O	H	O	O	H	O	O	O	H	O
O	H	O	O	H	O	H	O	H	O	H	O	O
H	O	H	O	O	H	O	H	O	H	O	O	O
O	O	H	H	O	O	O	H	H	O	O	O	H
H	O	H	O	O	H	O	O	O	H	H	O	O
O	H	O	O	H	H	H	O	O	H	O	O	O
O	O	H	H	O	O	H	O	H	H	O	O	O
H	H	O	O	O	O	O	H	O	H	H	H	O
O	O	H	H	O	O	O	H	H	O	O	H	O
H	O	H	H	O	O	H	H	O	O	O	O	H
H	H	O	O	H	H	O	O	O	O	H	O	O

O	O	H	H	H	O	H	O	O	H	O
H	O	H	H	O	H	O	H	O	O	H
O	H	O	O	H	O	O	H	O	O	O
O	H	O	O	H	O	H	O	H	O	H
H	O	H	O	O	H	O	H	O	H	O
O	O	H	H	O	O	O	H	H	O	O
H	O	H	O	O	H	O	O	O	H	H
O	H	O	O	H	H	H	O	O	H	O
O	O	H	H	O	O	H	O	H	H	O
H	H	O	O	O	O	O	H	O	H	H
O	O	H	H	O	O	O	H	H	O	O
H	O	H	H	O	O	H	H	O	O	O
H	H	O	O	H	H	O	O	O	O	H
O	H	O	O	H	O	H	O	H	H	O
H	O	H	O	H	O	O	H	O	O	H
H	O	H	H	O	H	O	H	O	O	H
H	O	H	O	O	H	O	H	O	H	O

Now that you're a water-making pro, try your hand at some salt (one sodium and one chloride). Here's the trick: One sodium is Na and one chloride is Cl. You have to connect two letters just to make one atom.

The first salt molecule has been found. How many more can you locate in this sample game?

N	C	A	L
N	A	A	C
C	L	L	N
N	C	L	C
A	L	N	A

Grid 1:

N	N	C	A	L	N	A	L	C	L	A
A	A	L	L	N	A	C	C	L	A	N
C	L	N	C	A	L	C	A	N	A	L
L	C	A	N	A	C	A	C	N	A	N
N	A	N	A	C	N	L	A	A	C	N
C	A	L	N	N	L	A	N	C	A	A
N	A	N	N	A	L	L	N	C	A	N
A	A	N	C	L	A	C	A	A	A	C
L	L	N	L	A	L	C	A	C	L	N
L	N	L	A	L	C	L	C	N	A	L
N	C	A	C	L	C	N	C	A	C	L
A	N	A	L	N	A	N	A	C	N	A
L	N	A	N	C	N	L	A	A	N	C
A	N	L	C	N	A	C	L	N	A	L
C	N	A	L	C	N	L	N	A	L	C
A	L	N	A	L	C	L	A	C	N	A

Grid 2:

A	N	C	A	L	N	L	L	C	N	A	A
L	A	L	N	N	A	C	C	L	A	L	C
C	L	N	C	A	L	N	C	A	C	C	L
N	A	N	N	A	L	L	A	C	A	N	A
A	A	N	N	C	N	C	A	N	C	N	A
N	A	L	N	N	L	A	N	C	C	N	A
A	A	N	A	C	N	C	L	N	N	A	L
N	C	A	L	A	C	A	C	N	L	N	A
C	N	C	C	L	A	A	N	N	A	C	C
L	N	A	C	C	N	L	N	A	C	L	L
C	C	A	L	L	L	C	C	C	A	N	C
L	N	A	A	A	N	N	C	A	A	L	N
N	N	A	C	C	N	N	N	A	L	N	L
C	N	L	L	N	A	A	L	N	L	L	C
L	L	N	N	A	L	L	A	C	L	L	C
A	L	N	A	L	C	N	A	C	A	A	L

Animals may not have language like humans do, but they do communicate by moving their bodies, making noises, and even releasing smells or flashing colors. What are the animals below trying to tell you?

THE BALLAD OF PLUTO

Once upon a time, our solar system had nine planets: Mercury, Venus, Earth, Mars, Jupiter, Saturn, Uranus, Neptune, and Pluto. But in 2005, a group of scientists called the International Astronomical Union decided that Pluto just wasn't big enough to be a planet. Now our solar system has only eight. In order to honor the planet that is no longer a planet, write a ballad to Pluto. A ballad is a poem or song that tells a story, usually sad. Below are some lines to write in, and some helpful facts about Pluto to get you started.

- **Pluto was discovered in 1930 by Clyde W. Tombaugh (rhymes with dumbo—sort of).**

- **Pluto has a weird orbit, so sometimes it gets closer to the sun than Neptune, even though it's usually farthest from the sun.**

- **An 11-year-old girl named Venetia Burney came up with the name "Pluto," which was also the name of the Roman god of the underworld.**

- **Pluto's surface is covered in ice.**

_____

_____

_____

_____

_____

TWO TRUTHS AND A LIE

How much do you know about the people who made all of the amazing discoveries and crazy inventions you learn about in school? Test your knowledge with this game. Each scientist will tell you three things about themselves, but one of them is a lie. See if you can figure out which one. **Answers on page 143.**

Albert Einstein

Hi, my name is Albert. I taught myself to play all of Mozart's sonatas on the violin, I came up with the theory of relativity, and I had few friends as a child because I got such good grades in school.

What's the lie?

_____

_____

Rachel Carson

Hi, I'm Rachel. My book *Silent Spring* helped to start the modern environmental movement. I always liked writing, and I had a story published when I was 10 years old. I was also a black belt in karate.

What's the lie?

_____

Neil DeGrasse Tyson

Hello. I'm Neil, and when I was in high school, I was the captain of my school's wrestling team. When I'm not studying astronomy, I spend my time raising llamas on a farm. I also make lots of guest appearances on TV shows like *The Big Bang Theory* and *Who Wants to Be a Millionaire?*

What's the lie?

Mae Carol Jemison

My name is Mae, and I was the first African-American woman to travel in space. I also appeared in an episode of *Star Trek: The Next Generation*, and I am a licensed pilot, so I can fly airplanes.

What's the lie?

Marie Curie

My name is Marie. I played seven instruments, including the guitar and the mandolin. I don't want to brag, but I was the first person to ever win two Nobel Prizes, and the first woman to win any. During World War I, I helped soldiers by creating mobile X-ray machines.

What's the lie?

Ukichiro Nakaya

Hello, my name is Ukichiro. I created the first artificial snowflake—you could say I'm a pretty *cool* guy. I was well-known for being an amazing skier. I also did a type of ink wash painting known as sumi-e.

What's the lie?

_____

_____

_____

Franz Boas

Hi, I'm Franz, but my friends call me "the Father of American Anthropology" (anthropology means the study of humans). Some early anthropologists believed that some cultures were better than others, but I believed in cultural relativism, which means that cultures aren't better or worse than each other—they're just different. I studied cultures all over the world, but mostly in Europe. I was a great teacher, and many of my students became famous anthropologists, too.

What's the lie?

_____

Omar Khayyam

My name is Omar. I was a mathematician and scientists during the Islamic Golden Age, a time period in the Middle Ages when science flourished in the Islamic world. I did many cool things, even using math and astronomy to improve the calendar. Not to mention that, I invented the telescope!

What's the lie?

_____

Nikola Tesla

Hello, I'm Nikola. I became famous as an inventor because I developed a new kind of electrical system. Even though I was pretty rich, I spent my whole life living in hotels. My best friend was my cat, Edison.

What's the lie?

_____

Galileo Galilei

Hey, I'm Galileo, the father of science. I gave up a promising career as a concert pianist to pursue science. Unfortunately, I was put under house arrest because I believed the Earth rotated around the sun (which it does!). And guess what? The four largest moons of Jupiter are named after me.

What's the lie?

_____

TAKE ME TO YOUR LEADER

Aliens have just landed in your backyard, and they want to know as much as possible about the inhabitants of Earth.

What do the aliens look like? Draw them!

What does their spacecraft look like? Draw it.

Why have they come to Earth?

_____

_____

_____

They want to meet the five most important people in the world. Who do you take them to see?

1. _____

2. _____

3. _____

4. _____

5. _____

They are hungry. What will you feed them?

Dinner:

_____
_____
_____
_____
_____

Dessert:

_____
_____
_____
_____
_____

They want to know about human history. What five events do you tell them about?

1. _____

2. _____

3. _____

4. _____

5. _____

What five movies do you show them?

1. _____

2. _____

3. _____

4. _____

5. _____

What five locations around the world do you take them to?

1. _____

2. _____

3. _____

4. _____

5. _____

What five books do you give them to read?

1. _____

2. _____

3. _____

4. _____

5. _____

They are thinking of taking over Earth from the humans. What arguments for or against this idea can you come up with?

Five arguments for conquest:

1. _____

2. _____

3. _____

4. _____

5. _____

Five arguments against conquest:

1. _____

2. _____

3. _____

4. _____

5. _____

SCI-FI WORKSHOP

Science fiction (or sci-fi) is a genre where people write about things that aren't real but are based on real science, meaning they could be real someday. Sometimes, real scientific discoveries come from science fiction ideas (like robots). Use the prompts below to write some short science fiction of your own. For each section, write a story that includes the character, object, and action provided.

Ornithologist, LASER, discover

_____

_____

_____

_____

_____

_____

_____

_____

_____

_____

_____

_____

_____

_____

Extraterrestrial, telescope, experiment

Professor, hydrogen, catastrophe

Robot, human race, save

_____

_____

_____

_____

_____

_____

_____

_____

_____

_____

_____

_____

_____

_____

WHAT IS YOUR SCIENTIST NAME?

Most scientists seem to have pretty normal names, like Albert Einstein. But scientists are so cool, we think they should all change their names to things like Pythagoras Lightningrod. Let's start with you. Use your birth month and day to figure out what your super secret awesome science name is.

January- Arctic
February- Mercury
March- Hydrogenation
April- Copernicus
May- Hubble
June- Electricity

July- Carbon Cycle
August- Ionic
September- Predator
October- Frankenstein
November- Deciduous
December- Tsunami

1- Laserbeam
2- Tundra
3- Smartypants
4- Plutonium
5- Treeclimber
6- Insectivore
7- Anthropologer
8- Phlogiston
9- Catastrophus
10- Rocketblast
11- The Observant
12- Codebreaker
13- Einstein
14- Weatherman
15- Galaxy
16- The Nutrient Dense

17- Mythbuster
18- Knowledge
19- Linnaeus
20- Wormhole
21- Sapiens
22- Taxonomer
23- Catalyst
24- Mathematicus
25- Arthropod
26- Igneous
27- Vapor
28- Ammonia
29- Volcano
30- Labcoat
31- Fibula

What's your scientist name?

_____

How about your friends and family?

_____
_____
_____
_____
_____
_____
_____
_____
_____
_____

You can make your name even cooler by adding a title like "Lord" or "Queen" in front of it.

_____
_____
_____

DEFYING GRAVITY

Have you ever wondered why things fall when you drop them? The answer is gravity, which is a very strong force that controls everything from you on a trampoline to the planets and stars. But what if there was no gravity? Draw some things that are no longer controlled by gravity.

DEBUNKED!

Sometimes, scientists discover things that just aren't true. Other scientists prove them wrong later, and sometimes those discoveries seem silly when we look back on them. But if scientists didn't try and fail, we would never have the amazing discoveries like gravity that turned out to be true after all. To help show some respect to debunked ideas, we've put together a graveyard. Write some tasteful epitaphs for science gone wrong.

Example epitaph: Here lies an idea that didn't pass on to its descendants

Lamarckian Evolution

Lamarck was a smart guy—he believed evolution existed even before Darwin! Unfortunately, he also thought that evolution happened because every time an animal changed, it passed that change on to its descendants. But if that were true, a parent who broke her arm would have kids with broken arms!

Alchemy

A really long time ago, scientists called alchemists believed that they could turn less valuable metals into gold. If it sounds impossible, that's because it is. But that kind of thinking is what led scientists to mess around with chemicals, leading to the field of chemistry which people still study today.

Geocentric Universe

Before a scientist named Copernicus proved otherwise, everyone believed that the earth was the center of the entire universe. Really, we're just a tiny speck in the middle of nowhere.

Vulcan

Some scientists in the 1800s thought that there had to be a planet between Mercury and the Sun, which they called Vulcan (the same name as the Roman god of fire—probably because a planet so close to the sun would have been really hot). Even though lots of people claimed to have seen the planet, it was proved to not exist.

Phlogiston

The scientist Johan Becher wondered why some things could catch fire. He decided that all things able to burn must contain a mysterious substance called phlogiston that helped them catch on fire. There is only one flaw with this theory: there's no such thing as phlogiston.

MYSTERY WORDS

Figure out the mystery words below. For each letter, answer a science question. The first letter of the answer is the letter that goes in the corresponding box. **Answers on page 143.**

1	2	3	4	5	6	7

1. This element is used to stop other metals from rusting. It has the atomic number 30.

_____

2. This constellation was named after an enormous and strong hunter in Greek mythology.

_____

3. This sea creature has eight legs and is related to either snails or jellyfish.

_____

4. This predator lives in the same habitat as giraffes and acacia trees.

_____

5. This scientist lived during the Islamic Golden Age, and he may or may not have invented the telescope.

_____

6. This force holds planets in their orbit and keeps you from floating into the sky.

_____

7. This person could be a scientist some day. Hint: Look in a mirror.

1	2	3	4	5	6	7	8	9	10

1. This scientist figured out that $E = MC^2$, and he was a fan of the violin.

_____

2. You can use this invention to see far away things, like the stars, a little bit closer.

_____

3. This planet, unlike Vulcan, is the closest planet to the sun.

_____

4. In this habitat, you might find fish, sharks, and even scuba divers.

_____

5. This is what our book is about!

_____

6. People with this scientific job help treat mental illnesses.

_____

7. This is the element you put in a balloon to make it float. It has the atomic number 2.

_____

8. This is the tallest mountain the world.

_____

9. This is what a geologist studies.

_____

10. This was Charles Darwin's famous idea.

_____

Create some mystery word puzzles for friends to solve.

1	2	3	4	5	6	7	8	9	10

1. _____

_____

2. _____

_____

3. _____

_____

4. _____

_____

5. _____

_____

6. _____

_____

7. _____

_____

8. _____

_____

9. _____

_____

10. _____

_____

1	2	3	4	5	6	7	8	9	10

1. _____

_____

2. _____

_____

3. _____

_____

4. _____

_____

5. _____

_____

6. _____

_____

7. _____

_____

8. _____

_____

9. _____

_____

10. _____

_____

WEIRD WEATHER

There are all kinds of weather—tornadoes, thunderstorms, tsunamis, sunny days, hurricanes, plain old rain. But sometimes, weather does things you would never expect. For example, waterspouts can pick up animals like fish or frogs, carry them miles away, and drop them on the ground like rain. Draw what's falling from the clouds below.

CONSTELLATION CREATOR

For thousands of years, humans have looked up at the sky and seen shapes. These shapes are called constellations, and they all have stories behind them, like the giant hunter Orion or his enemy, Scorpio. There are a bunch of stars on page 58. Connect the dots to create some constellations of your own, and then name them here and tell us who or what they are.

1. **Name of constellation:** _____

Its story:

_____

_____

_____

_____

_____

2. **Name of constellation:** _____

Its story:

_____

_____

_____

_____

_____

3. Name of constellation: _____

Its story:

_____

_____

_____

_____

_____

4. Name of constellation: _____

Its story:

_____

_____

_____

_____

_____

5. Name of constellation: _____

Its story:

_____

_____

_____

_____

_____

PANGAEA

Did you know that all the continents on earth used to be connected in one big supercontinent called *pangaea*? Below are all the continents as they are today. On the following page, see if you can draw them all together into pangaea again.

RADIATION SENSATION

A German scientist named Wilhelm Röntgen made X-rays famous in the late 1800s when he took a picture of his wife's hand that showed the bones inside it. Today, anyone can get an X-ray at the doctor to reveal a broken bone or a swallowed penny. The creatures on the next few pages are getting X-rayed. Can you draw what's inside of them?

RORSCHACH TEST

Some psychologists use pictures of inkblots to figure out what people are thinking. Have a friend look at the inkblots below and tell you what they think they are. Then, try and interpret their answers. For example, if they say they see a chicken leg, you can tell them they might be hungry.

What your friend saw:

_____

_____

_____

What your friend saw:

_____

_____

_____

Your interpretation:

_____

_____

_____

Your interpretation:

_____

_____

_____

What your friend saw:

_____

_____

_____

_____

_____

What your friend saw:

_____

_____

_____

_____

Your interpretation:

_____

_____

_____

_____

_____

Your interpretation:

_____

_____

_____

_____

_____

What your friend saw:

_____

_____

_____

_____

_____

What your friend saw:

_____

_____

_____

_____

_____

Your interpretation:

_____

_____

_____

_____

_____

Your interpretation:

_____

_____

_____

_____

_____

What your friend saw: **What your friend saw:**

_____

_____

_____

_____

_____

Your interpretation: **Your interpretation:**

_____

_____

_____

_____

_____

SCIENCE WORD GRID

Try to fill in the grid with science words using the following rules.

- You can play alone, or with as many people as you like.

- The goal is to find as many words as possible to fit in each square of the grid. The words must fit with the category and letter of the grid. See the example in the first square (a plant beginning with the letter P).

- A player gets a point for every original word they come up with.

- Whoever has the most points when nobody can think of any more words, wins.

	Plants	Animals	Types of Scientists	Things in Space
P	Petunia			
L				
U				
T				
O				

	Plants	Animals	Types of Scientists	Things in Space
P	Petunia			
L				
U				
T				
O				

	Plants	Animals	Types of Scientists	Things in Space
P	Petunia			
L				
U				
T				
O				

	Jobs That Use Science	Weather Words	Diseases & Illnesses	Types of Machines
S				
A				
T				
U				
R				
N				

	Jobs That Use Science	Weather Words	Diseases & Illnesses	Types of Machines
S				
A				
T				
U				
R				
N				

	Jobs That Use Science	Weather Words	Diseases & Illnesses	Types of Machines
S				
A				
T				
U				
R				
N				

	Jobs That Use Science	Weather Words	Diseases & Illnesses	Types of Machines
S				
A				
T				
U				
R				
N				

MOUNTAIN MANIA

Mountains are formed when the many tectonic plates—or big slabs of rock—that form the surface of the Earth crash into each other and create big bumps, whether it's the Appalachian mountains in the United States or Mount Everest, the tallest mountain in the world. Below there is a mountain range, but it's your job to draw what's going on underneath it. Add tectonic plates, magma, and maybe some things that don't really belong there, like dwarves and pirates.

PERSONALITY TEST

Psychologists are scientists who study how human minds work. Some psychologists believe that human personalities can be broken down into five main traits: openness to experience, conscientiousness, extroversion, agreeableness, and neuroticism. They theorize that every person falls somewhere on a scale of each trait. To find out what kind of personality you might have, take this short quiz. Remember, quizzes like this aren't perfect, and this one's just for fun, so don't take it too seriously.

1. I worry about things.
   a. Strongly agree
   b. Agree
   c. Disagree
   d. Strongly disagree

2. I am very imaginative.
   a. Strongly agree
   b. Agree
   c. Disagree
   d. Strongly disagree

3. I talk to lots of people at school.
   a. Strongly agree
   b. Agree
   c. Disagree
   d. Strongly disagree

4. I understand things quickly.
   a. Strongly agree
   b. Agree
   c. Disagree
   d. Strongly disagree

5. I feel others' emotions.
   a. Strongly agree
   b. Agree
   c. Disagree
   d. Strongly disagree

6. I like to be the center of attention.
   a. Strongly agree
   b. Agree
   c. Disagree
   d. Strongly disagree

7. I get stressed out easily.
   a. Strongly agree
   b. Agree
   c. Disagree
   d. Strongly disagree

8. I make time for other people.
   a. Strongly agree
   b. Agree
   c. Disagree
   d. Strongly disagree

9. I like to make sure everything is perfect.
   a. Strongly agree
   b. Agree
   c. Disagree
   d. Strongly disagree

10. I am easily distracted.
   a. Strongly agree
   b. Agree
   c. Disagree
   d. Strongly disagree

What Your Answers Say About You

Openness to experience: If you answered a or b for questions 2 and 4, you are more inventive and curious. You may not like routines, and you are independent. If you answered c or d for these questions, you are more consistent. You try and achieve things by persevering, and you are more practical.

Conscientiousness: If you answered a or b for question 9, you are thoughtful with good impulse control and can set goals. If you answered a or b for question 10, you may have trouble getting organized and paying attention to details.

Extroversion: If you answered a or b for questions 3 and 6, you are more of an extrovert. You are energized by spending time with other people and you seek out exciting situations. If you answered c or d, you are more introverted. You may love being social, but you also need to spend some time alone to recharge. Quiet activities are exciting for you.

Agreeableness: If you answered a or b for questions 5 and 8, you care more about getting along with other people. Being polite and friendly is important to you. If you answered c or d, you are more competitive.

Neuroticism: If you answered a or b for questions 1 and 7, you tend to be more sensitive and vulnerable. If you answered c or d, you seek out stability, and may appear to be more confident.

MARS UP CLOSE

People used to think Mars was inhabited by Martians.
What do you think is on Mars?

DREAM HOUSE FOR THE ENVIRONMENT

Most of the world uses oil, coal, and other non-renewable sources to create energy for electricity, cars, and other needs. Unfortunately, these fossil fuels are very bad for the environment and are a key contributor to climate change. Let's make the home below a little more environmentally friendly using the methods described on page 81.

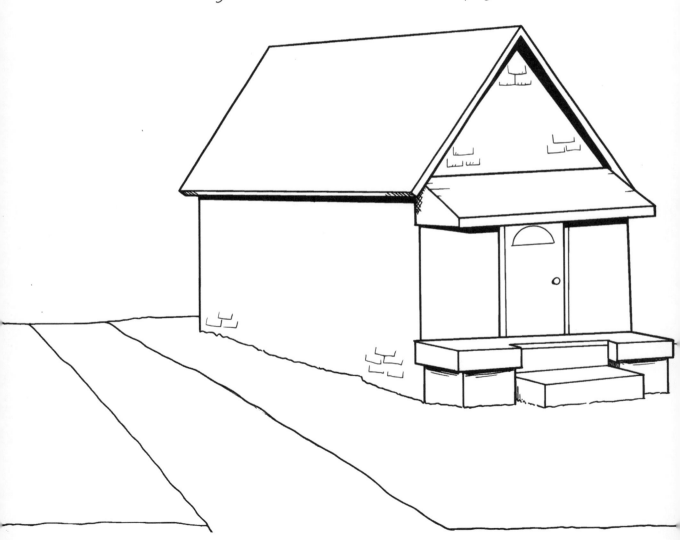

Solar Panels— The roof of this house is looking a little bare. Luckily, you can decorate it with solar panels. Solar panels look kind of like grids of mirrors. They collect sunlight (a resource that never runs out) and use it to create electricity and heat water.

Drought-Resistant Yard— Grass and flowers can be pretty, but in hot places with little water, keeping a yard like that uses up a lot of water that is needed for drinking and other purposes. Even though it can seem like it, there isn't an endless amount of water in the world, and some people don't have enough to drink. You can help by drawing some cacti and a rock garden for a yard. Get creative!

Windows— Every house has windows, but having the right kind of windows is important. It's best to put windows on the east and south sides of the house. That way, your house will stay cool in the summer and warm in the winter. If you don't know which way east and south are, check the compass below.

Bicycle— Instead of a car, draw some other modes of transportation in the driveway. Whether you use a bike, a trike, or a pogo stick, anything is better than a gas-guzzling car. Of course, some people live too far from cities to get around without a car. Draw them an energy-efficient car, or even an electric one of your own design.

Rain Barrel— It's important to save water. Luckily, in many places, water falls right from the sky. Draw a barrel beside the house to collect rainwater that can be used to water plants and for other water-related tasks.

Know of any environmentally friendly tricks that aren't included here? Feel free to draw them, even if you have to invent them first.

OBSERVING THE WORLD AROUND YOU

One very important thing that scientists do is observe things around them so they can come up with questions to test and theories about the world. Some observe how monkeys behave in the wild, or how certain chemicals act when they're mixed together. But right now, you can just observe the things around you, in your bedroom, the car, or wherever you are. List your observations below, and write what they might mean.

Example:

There are colorful handprints on the walls...
My little sister is finger painting again!

_____   _____
                                 _____
_____   _____
                                 _____
_____   _____
                                 _____
_____   _____
                                 _____
_____   _____
                                 _____
_____   _____

_____   _____
                                     _____
_____   _____
                                     _____
_____   _____
                                     _____
                                     _____
_____   _____
                                     _____
                                     _____
_____   _____
                                     _____
                                     _____
_____   _____
                                     _____
_____   _____
                                     _____

PLAYING WITH GENES

Scientists can mess around with genes and DNA to create things that don't exist in nature, like featherless chickens and glow-in-the-dark mice. Think about what kinds of creatures you could create this way. A frog-donkey? An elephant-sized fly? Draw some of your ideas on these pages.

CREATE YOUR OWN ELEMENT

When scientists discover elements, they get to give them cool names like Francium and Curium. But today, you get to do something even better: Create your own element!

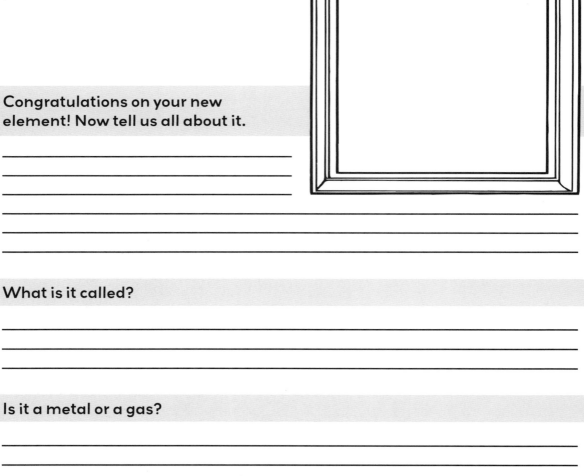

Congratulations on your new element! Now tell us all about it.

_____
_____
_____
_____
_____
_____

What is it called?

_____
_____
_____

Is it a metal or a gas?

_____
_____
_____

At room temperature, is it liquid, solid, or gas?

_____

_____

_____

How hot does it have to be to melt?

_____

_____

_____

What are some of its cool properties?

_____

_____

_____

What is it used for?

_____

_____

_____

What is its atomic symbol? (i.e., H or Pb)

_____

_____

_____

How did you discover it?

_____

_____

_____

_____

ROCKIN' OUT

There are three main types of rock: igneous, sedimentary, and metamorphic. Below is a cool tune about them, but some words are missing. See if you can fill in the blanks, and then start a sing-along with your friends, family, and pets! Clues appear on the opposite page. **Answers are on page 144.**

Sing along to the tune of _Twinkle, Twinkle Little Star_!

A rock is formed when (1) _____ cools,
Made of different molecules.
This rock is called (2) _____,
And it's pretty serious.
It keeps our planet wrapped up tight
(3) _____, basalt, and diorite.

This new rock is (4) _____,
From sediment to sedimentary.
Rocks get crushed beneath the ocean
(5) _____ sets the process in motion.
Before you know you've got a whole new stone,
Limestone, sandstone, shale or (6) _____.

Some kinds of rock just like to change.
Under (7) _____ they rearrange.
Deep down underneath the ground
Metamorphic rock is found
Any (8) _____ can get its shape garbled
And become slate, gneiss or (9) _____.

Clues:

1. Similar to lava

2. It rhymes!

3. A type of hard rock that you shouldn't take for GRANTED

4. Your first few years of school

5. Lots of weight that PRESSES down on you

6. You can burn it for energy

7. High temperatures

8. Stone

9. Think of small glass balls you can play games with

MAD SCIENTIST

Scientists are always asking "Why?" Why do volcanoes explode? Why do dogs chase their tails? Why do we have nose hair? With this game, you can provide scientific answers. The only problem is you won't know the questions ahead of time.

- **Rip out the game cards on the next few pages. If you have more players than cards, make of some your own with scrap paper.**

- **Have each player write down a question beginning with "Why."**

- **Fold the game cards to hide the question.**

- **Pass your card to the next person, who, without looking at the question, writes an answer.**

- **When you're done, read out questions and answers.**

Question

Why

_____
_____
_____
_____
_____
_____

Answers

Because

_____
_____
_____
_____
_____
_____

Question

Why

_____
_____
_____
_____
_____
_____

Answers

Because

_____
_____
_____
_____
_____
_____

Question

Why

_____
_____
_____
_____
_____
_____

Answers

Because

_____
_____
_____
_____
_____
_____

Question

Why

_____
_____
_____
_____
_____
_____

Answers

Because

_____
_____
_____
_____
_____
_____

Question

Why

_____
_____
_____
_____
_____
_____

Answers

Because

_____
_____
_____
_____
_____
_____

Question

Why

_____
_____
_____
_____
_____
_____

Answers

Because

_____
_____
_____
_____
_____
_____

Question

Why

_____
_____
_____
_____
_____
_____

Answers

Because

_____
_____
_____
_____
_____

Question

Why

_____
_____
_____
_____
_____
_____

Answers

Because

_____
_____
_____
_____
_____

WHO ATE MY TRASH?

Even though it might seem gross to us, plenty of animals like to eat the stuff we throw out. Your trash can was raided last night, and you found some footprints that might lead you to the culprit. Unfortunately, there are footprints from all different kinds of animals. Take a look at the guide below, then turn the page and try to figure out who did it without looking at the guide.

Answers on page 144.

Guide

Raccoon: Raccoon prints look like little hands with claws. Raccoons come out at night to look for food that they pick up with their front paws. They eat fish, eggs, fruit, and are notorious for stealing human garbage.

Squirrel: Squirrel tracks are long and thin, with five fingers lined up beside each other. They eat all kinds of nuts as well as fruit and seeds. While they won't turn their nose up at the half sandwich you drop on the ground, they're a little small for knocking over trash cans.

Black Bear: Black Bear prints are large with an almost triangular palm and five short toes with long claws. In the wild, these bears eat fruit, grass, insects, and sometimes fish. But when their habitats are invaded by humans, they can get used to eating human trash, which isn't good for them or the humans.

Coyote: Coyote tracks might look a little like dog prints. They have a small triangular palm and four clawed toes. Coyotes will eat animals such as rabbits, mice, and squirrels, and will also scavenge animals killed by other predators. When they're stuck in urban settings, however, they will eat trash.

LAB WORK

What's in and/or coming out of these vials and test tubes?

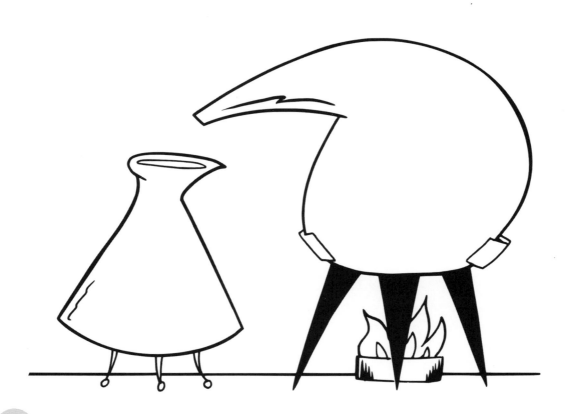

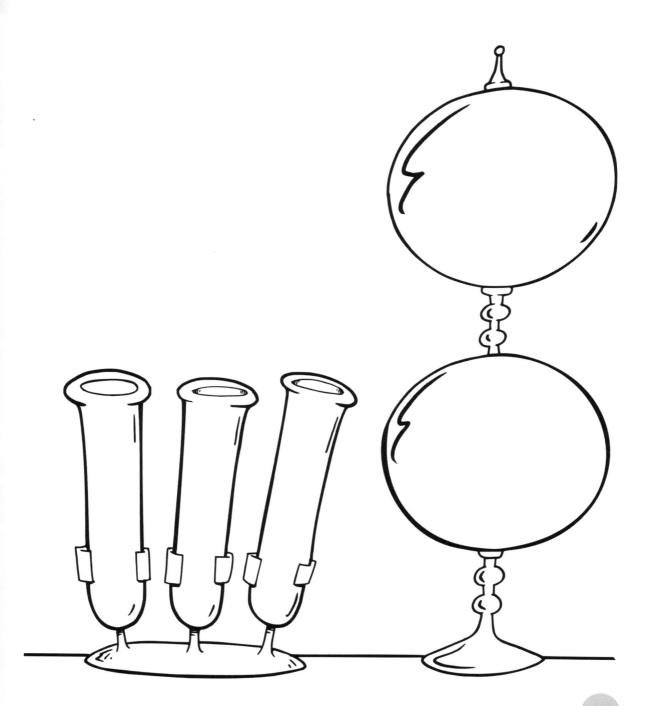

FOOD CHAIN

You've probably heard of predators (meat-eating animals that eat other animals), but did you know that in every ecosystem, there is an entire chain of animals and plants, all eating each other? This is called a food chain. For example, a shark might eat a big fish that eats a little fish that eats underwater plants.

Can you doodle the following food chains—as if they were all about to eat each other at the same time?

Grass — Grasshopper — Rat — Snake — Hawk

Algae — Krill — Cod fish — Seal — Killer Whale

Leaves — Mouse — Rabbit — Jackal — Lion

Come up with your own food chain here:

EINSTEIN'S HAIR

Albert Einstein developed the general theory of relativity and received the Nobel Prize in Physics in 1921. He also had wild hair. Give the people and animals below Einstein hair.

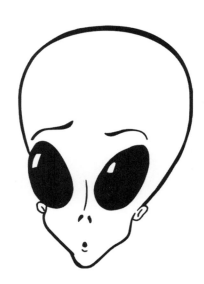

ANIMAL PUNS

Use the animals below to complete the puns on the following page.
Answers on page 144.

1.

2.

3.

4.

5.

6.

7.

8.

9.

10.

1. Don't listen to Lisa. She's _____.

2. Mom's bad mood is becoming un _____able.

3. It's okay if you're running late. _____wait.

4. In order to run in the final race, Jason needs to _____fy first.

5. Tomorrow's our last day of vacation. _____ my things in the morning.

6. Have a safe trip. Let _____ when you get there.

7. Your new shoes are _____ally awesome.

8. These puns are the _____iest things I've ever heard.

9. The teacher doesn't know how to control his class. It's complete _____monium.

10. I hope you found these puns a _____ing.

Come up with some of your own animal puns here:

11.

_____

12.

_____

13.

_____

14.

_____

15.

_____

THE LOGY QUIZ

The suffix -logy means a branch of learning or study. It is used with other words or root words to name the different sciences. Bio + logy = the study of living organisms. How much do you know about the different types of sciences out there?

Answers on page 144.

1. Hippology is the study of:

A. Horses
B. Joints
C. Hippopotamuses
D. All of the above

2. Which -logy is the study of fish?

A. Immunology
B. Neurology
C. Oceanology
D. Ichthyology

3. Is the study of teeth odonatology or odontology?

4. Rhinology is the study of:

A. Rhinoceroses
B. Noses
C. Horns
D. Fingernails

5. The study of poop is called:

A. Poopology
B. Feceology
C. Scatology
D. There is no such science

6. Is the study of sleep called somnology or dendrology?

7. If you were an exobiologist, you would be studying:

    A. Life in outer space
    B. The human skeleton
    C. Microscopic life found in dirt
    D. Cellular disagreements

8. True or False: There is a branch of science that studies flags.

9. If your head is always in the clouds, you might be a/an:

    A. Mistologist
    B. Cumulologist
    C. Nephologist
    D. Daydreamologist

10. Do you like playing video games? Perhaps you should become a:

    A. Videologist
    B. Ludologist
    C. X-boxologist
    D. Oologist

ELEMENT WARS

It's time for an epic battle—chemistry style. Grab a friend and get ready to defeat them using only the elements.

Each player starts out with 20 points. Before the game begins, players take turns choosing which elements they would like to have as weapons and defenses.

Tear out the page of element cards and carefully tear each one out individually.

The player who took the second turn choosing element cards goes first. They select a card from their hand and use it to attack their opponent. After the card is used it is placed to the side. With each attack, the defending player may either absorb the attack (and lose the amount of points specified on the card) or deflect it with a defensive card. Each defense card may deflect a portion or the whole of the inflicted damage (for example, if a card that can deflect 5 damage points is used against a card that inflicts 7 damage points, the defensive player will receive 2 damage points).

During each turn, a player may choose to forfeit their turn and take a card from the discard pile instead. They can then use this card to attack or defend during any following turn. This is an important part of the game, as it keeps the game from ending too quickly.

When one player has no remaining points, the other player wins.

Silver

Helps you stay healthy by killing bacteria, fungi, and yeast

Deflect 4 damage points

Fluorine

A poisonous gas

Inflict 4 damage points

Copper

Conducts electricity very well

Zap your opponent
Inflict 4 damage points

Francium

One of the most radioactive elements

Inflict 8 damage points

Beryllium

Has such a low density it is transparent on X-rays

Become invisible and dodge an attack
Deflect 5 damage points

Lead

Used to stop radioactive gamma rays

Play to block a radioactivity attack
Deflect 8 damage points

Hydrogen

Very flammable

Play to blast your opponent
Inflict 7 damage points

Liquid Nitrogen

It freezes whatever it touches.

Play to freeze your opponent
Inflict 6 damage points

Iridium

Iridium can not be easily corroded by anything.

Play to block small attacks
Deflect 5 damage points

Krypton

Used in LASERs

Play to attack with LASER beams.

Inflict 5 damage points

Arsenic

Poisonous to humans.

Play to infect your opponent with toxicity

Inflict 4 damage points

Nitrogen

Used in bullet-proof vests

Play to deflect an attack

Deflect 3 damage points

Sulfur

Many of its compounds stink

Inflict 2 damage points

Titanium

Strongest lightweight metal

Deflect 5 damage points

Bromine

Puts out fires

Deflect 4 damage points

Molybdenum

Used in strong metals and armor

Deflect 7 damage points

Plutonium

Used to make atomic bombs

Inflict 8 damage points

Uranium

Used to make nuclear weapons and armor-piercing bullets

Inflict 6 damage points

Use these blank playing cards to create more elements to use.

HYBRID HYSTERIA

A hybrid is the offspring of two plants or animals of different species or varieties. For instance, a mule is a hybrid of a donkey and a horse. Decide if the following hybrid combinations are real or fake, and draw what you think they'd look like.
Answers on page 144.

1. Cow + American Buffalo = Beefalo
Real or Fake

2. Hawk + Eagle = Hawkle
Real or Fake

3. Zebra + Horse = Zeedonk

Real or Fake

4. Dog + Wolf = Wog

Real or Fake

5. Lion + Tiger = Tigons

Real or Fake

6. Killer Whale + Dolphin = Wholphin
Real or Fake

7. Grizzly Bear + Polar Bear = Grolar Bear
Real or Fake

8. Sheep + Goat = Geep
Real or Fake

9. Shark + Minnow = Shinnow

Real or Fake

10. Gerbil + Hamster = Gerbster

Real or Fake

Use the next three pages to create and draw your own weird hybrid combinations of the following animals. Don't forget to give them cool names.

Elephant, Rhino, Hippopotamus, Deer, Anteater, Possum, Skunk, Antelope, Bear, Crow, Giraffe, Cat, Ferret, Camel, Cow, Shark, Electric Eel, Panda, Koala, and whatever else you can think of!

WOULD YOU RATHER: THE GERM EDITION

A germ is a microorganism that is capable of causing disease. As humans, we try to avoid germs so we can stay healthy. In this game, you have to choose the scenario that would lead to the least amount of germs. **Answers on page 144.**

1. Would you rather kiss a stranger or shake that person's hand?

_____

2. Would you rather lick a toilet seat or a smartphone?

_____

3. Would you rather kiss a cat or chew on a kitchen sponge?

_____

4. Would you rather go bowling or play miniature golf?

_____

5. Would you rather suck on a hotel remote control or your hotel bedspread?

_____

6. Would you rather share your toothbrush or your hairbrush?

_____

7. Would you rather lick your computer mouse or your computer keyboard?

_____

8. Would you rather have a sick person sneeze in your face or cough in your face?

_____

9. Would you rather eat your boogers for breakfast or never have any mucus (another word for boogers) in your nose at all?

_____

10. Would you rather play in the snow in a bathing suit or sit around a warm fireplace with your friends?

_____

BY THE NUMBERS

Each statement is missing a number. Choose the correct number from below. Each number is used only once.
Answers on page 144.

1. The speed of light is _____ miles per second.

2. The Earth is _____ billion years old.

3. The human eye blinks around _____ times a day.

4. A googol is the number 1 followed by _____ zeroes.

5. The average life expectancy of humans is around _____ years.

6. There are _____ miles of blood vessels in the human body.

7. It takes the light from the sun _____ minutes to travel to Earth.

100

7

29,000

2

71

2.2

8

60,000

8. There are _____ trillion galaxies in the universe.

9. There are _____ known elements.

10. There are more than _____ billion people on earth.

11. It would take _____ months to travel to Mars.

12. The closest galaxy to us is _____ million miles away.

13. The diameter of Earth at the equator is _____ miles.

14. The deepest known point in Earth's oceans is _____ feet below sea level.

15. The highest elevation above sea level on Earth is _____ feet.

6

4.56

7,926

29,035

36,000

186,000

115

THE GOLDEN RECORD

In 1977, two spacecraft, the Voyager 1 and 2, were sent into space to study the outer solar system and beyond. Both crafts also contained a Golden Record meant to communicate the human story to any extraterrestrials that may come upon it. The record contained sounds found in nature, music, images of daily life, and spoken greetings in dozens of languages. What would you put on your own Golden Record for aliens to find?

Nature sounds

1. _____

2. _____

3. _____

4. _____

5. _____

6. _____

7. _____

8. _____

9. _____

10. _____

11. _____

12. _____

13. _____

14. _____

15. _____

Songs

1. _____

2. _____

3. _____

4. _____

5. _____

6. _____

7. _____

8. _____

9. _____

10. _____

11. _____

12. _____

13. _____

14. _____

15. _____

Images

1. _____

2. _____

3. _____

4. _____

5. _____

6. _____

7. _____

8. _____

9. _____

10. _____

11. _____

12. _____

13. _____

14. _____

15. _____

MIX IT UP

Chemistry is the science of substances that make up everything and how these substance interact. Can you guess what happens if you combine the following substances with each other? Draw your results in the containers above the substances.
Answers on page 144.

Ammonia & Bleach

Mints & Diet Cola

Vinegar & Baking Soda

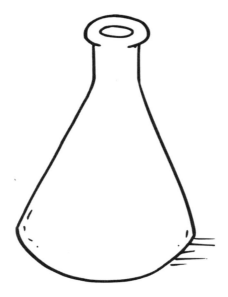

Laundry Detergent, Glue & Water

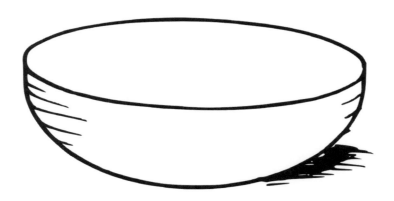

Ice Cream & Liquid Nitrogen

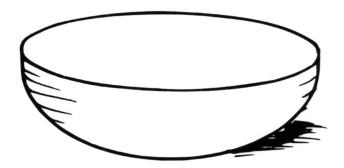

Hydrogen Peroxide, Yeast, Water & Dish Soap

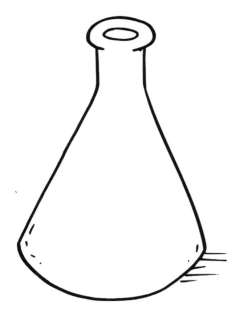

Heated Milk & Vinegar

Potassium & Water

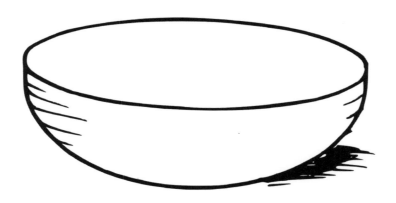

JUST HANGING OUT

Animals that spend a lot of their time in trees are called arboreal animals. Draw as many arboreal animals in these trees as you can.

CRAZY INVENTIONS

Everything around you was invented by someone who saw a problem and found a creative way to solve it. In order to get credit for an invention, you need to get it approved by the trademark office. In order to do that, you have to fill out an application and provide good reasons why your invention should be granted a patent. Many times, inventors include illustrations. The following illustrations come straight from real patent applications. (The numbers and arrows in many of these illustrations refer to written descriptions in the patents.) Let's have some fun with them.

What's raining down on this dog?

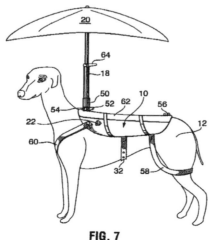

FIG. 7

Those tubes are for carrying around your rodent pets. Draw some gerbils and hamsters.

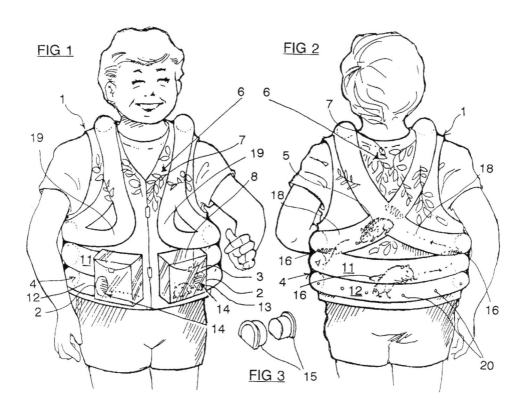

FIG 1

FIG 2

FIG 3

Invent a cool carrying case for pets here:

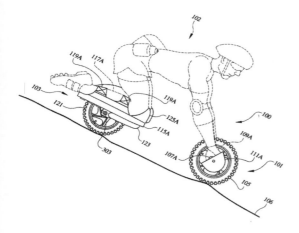

Create the rules for this game.

1. _____
_____

2. _____
_____

3. _____
_____

4. _____
_____

5. _____
_____

6. _____
_____

Fig. 1

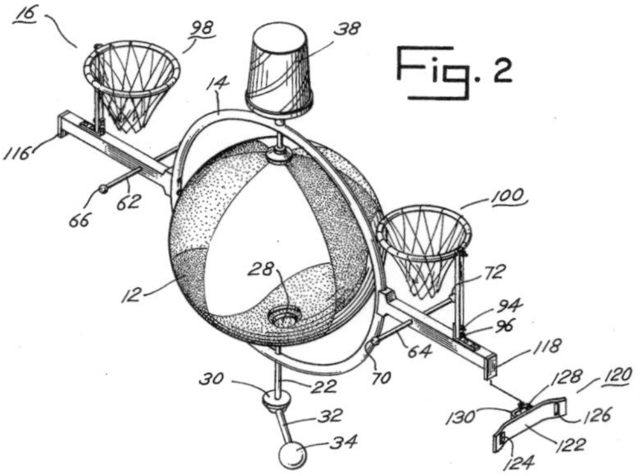

Fig. 2

Draw birds flying around this guy's head.

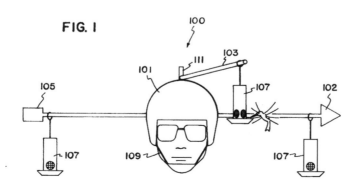

FIG. 1

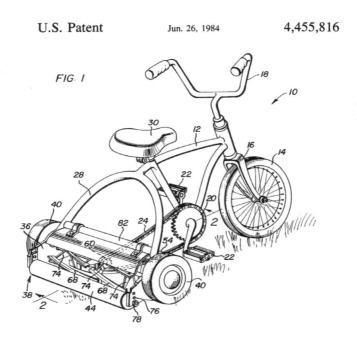

U.S. Patent   Jun. 26, 1984   4,455,816

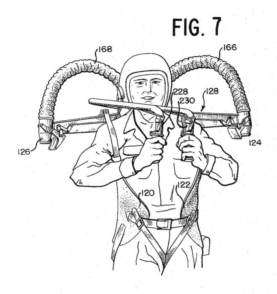

FIG. 7

Write a note to this guy telling him why his invention isn't going to work.

Dear _____,

_____

_____

_____

_____

_____

_____

_____

_____

_____

_____

_____

_____

_____

_____

_____

_____

_____

_____

_____

Fig. 1.

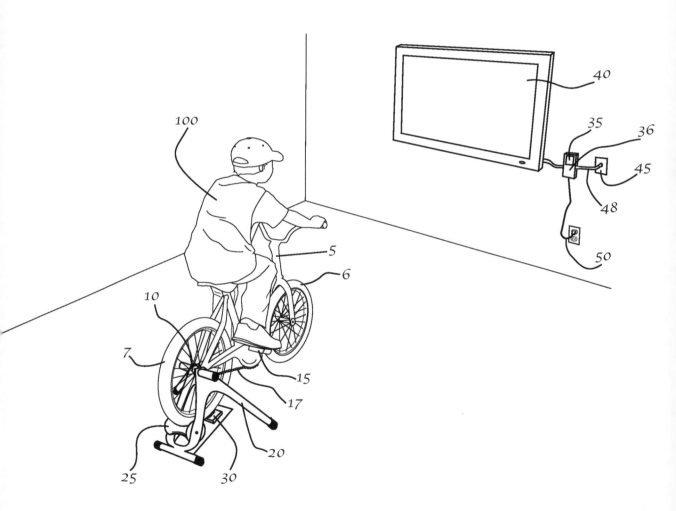

Draw some cool inventions here:

The Answers

Animal Cousins Answers (page 14)
1. Bird & dinosaur; 2. Whale & rhino;
3. Humans & lemurs; 4. Kangaroo & koala;
5. Crab & ladybug; 6. Sunflower & seaweed;
7. Turtle & alligator; 8. Camel & hippo;
9. Octopus & snail; 10. Hedgehog & mole

Scrambled Scientists Answers (page 16)
1. Pharmacist; 2. Biologist; 3. Professor;
4. Engineer; 5. Physicist; 6. Psychiatrist;
7. Meteorologist; 8. Environmentalist;
9. Geologist; 10. Botanist

Eureka! Answers (page 18)
Eureka!

a, are, ear, ere, rake, rue, ark, eke, auk, era, reek

It's alive!

a, ail, ails, aisle, ale, ales, alit, alive, as, at, ate, ates, ave, aves, east, eat, eats, evil, evils, I, isle, islet, it, its, ivies, last, lat, late, lats, lave, least, lei, leis, lest, let, lets, lev, liaise, lie, lies, list, lit, live, lives, sail, sale, salt, salve, sat, sate, save, sea, seal, seat, set, silt, silva, sit, site, slat, slate, slave, slit, stale, stave, steal, stile, tail, tails, tale, tales, tea, teal, teals, teas, tie, ties, til, tile, tiles, vail, vale, vales, valet, valets, valise, vase, vast, vat, vats, veal, veil, veils, vela, vest, vesta, vestal, vet, via, vial, vials, vie, vies, vile, vis, visa, vise, visit, vista, vita, vitae, vital, vitals

What's that?

a, ah, aha, as, ash, at, awash, ha, hah, has, hash, hat, hath, hats, haw, sat, saw, swat, swath, taw, taws, that, thats, thaw, thaws, twas, was, wash, watt, what

Yikes!

I, is, key, keys, sike, ski, sky, yes

Awesome!

a, am, as, awe, ease, ewe, ewes, ma, maw, maws, me, meow, mesa, mew, mews, mow, mows, ow, owe, owes, same, saw, sea, seam, see, seem, sew, so, soma, some, sow, swam, was, we, wee, woe, woes

Two Truths and a Lie Answers (page 30)
Albert Einstein: Okay, I lied about getting good grades. Actually, I hated school because my teachers wouldn't let me be creative. I got in trouble a lot.

Rachel Carson: Just kidding, I didn't do karate!

Neil DeGrasse Tyson: Unfortunately, I don't own llamas. But I am a dancer, a rower, as well as an astronomer.

Mae Carol Jemison: I may have stretched the truth about being a licensed pilot—but I am a licensed doctor.

Marie Curie: All right, I don't play seven instruments, I play three. Okay, I play two. Fine—none. I don't play any instruments.

Ukichiro Nakaya: I wasn't lying about loving snow—I took 3,000 photographs of snowflakes! But I never did learn to ski.

Franz Boas: Tricked you! I did study many human cultures, but I focused on indigenous tribes like the Inuit and never studied cultures in Europe.

Omar Khayyam: I didn't invent the telescope. That was a guy named Hans Lippershey. But I did write a cool treatise on algebra.

Nikola Tesla: I didn't have a cat, silly—they wouldn't let me bring him with me in all of those hotels! Also, I did NOT get along with the inventor Thomas Edison. I would not name a cat after him.

Galileo Galilei: It's possible that I was never a concert pianist.

Mystery Words Answers (page 50)
Word: Zoology
Questions: 1. Zinc; 2. Orion; 3. Octopus;
4. Lion; 5. Omar Khayyam; 6. Gravity;
7. You!
Fun fact: Zoology means the study of animals.

Word: Atmosphere
Questions: 1. Albert Einstein; 2. Telescope; 3. Mercury; 4. Ocean; 5. Science!; 6. Psychiatrist; 7. Helium; 8. Everest; 9. Rocks; 10. Evolution

Rockin' Out Answers (page 88)
1. Magma; 2. Igneous; 3. Granite; 4. Elementary; 5. Pressure; 6. Coal; 7. Heat; 8. Rock; 9. Marble

Who Ate My Trash Answer (page 95)
It was the raccoon.

Animal Puns Answers (page 104)
1. Lion; 2. Bear; 3. Owl; 4. Koala; 5. Alpaca; 6. Minnow; 7. Toad; 8. Seal; 9. Panda; 10. Moose

The Logy Quiz Answers (page 106)
1. A; 2. D; 3. Odontology (odonatology is the study of dragonflies); 4. B.; 5. C; 6. Somnology (dendrology is the study of trees); 7. A; 8. True (vexillology); 9. C.; 10. B (from the Latin word ludere, which means "to play")

Hybrid Hysteria Answers (page 115)
1. Real; 2. Fake; 3. Real; 4. Real; 5. Real; 6. Real; 7. Real; 8. Real; 9. Fake; 10. Fake

Would You Rather: The Germ Edition Answers (page 122)
1. More germs are transferred from shaking hands than from kissing. 2. A smartphone can have up to seven times more germs than a toilet seat. 3. Sponges can contain millions of germs while cats have far fewer. 4. A bowling alley will have more germs than a mini-golf course—think about all those fingers in the bowling balls! 5. Remote controls are teeming with germs! Bedspreads are washed often and have fewer germs. 6. More germs are spread by sharing a toothbrush... though watch out for lice! 7. Both are pretty germ-y; however, keyboards can have more than 3,000 germs per square inch while mouses only 1,600. 8. Either way, you've got tons of new germs to deal with. However, while coughing will send germs your way at around 50 miles an hour, a sneeze will shoot them at you at over 200 miles an hour. No time to duck! 9. Boogers (or mucus) are part of a defense system that wards off germs that are trying to enter your body. Some scientists say it may even be healthy to eat your boogers. However, without any mucus at all, your body would lose an important fighter of germs and you would most likely be sick more often. 10. If one of your friends has a cold or other virus, you could catch it by being close to them. Being really cold doesn't give you a cold.

By the Numbers Answers (page 124)
1. 186,000; 2. 4.56; 3. 29,000; 4. 100; 5. 71; 6. 60,000; 7. 8; 8. 2; 9. 115; 10. 7; 11. 6; 12. 2.2; 13. 7,926; 14. 36,000; 15. 29,035

Mix It Up Answers (page 128)
Ammonia & Bleach: Creates a poisonous gas cloud. The toxin created is chloramine vapor, which is extremely dangerous

Mints & Diet Cola: Cola shoots out of the bottle high into the sky. This is a reaction between the cola and mint that forcefully pushes most of the liquid out of the bottle.

Vinegar & Baking Soda: Creates foaming bubbles. Mixing these two together starts a chemical reaction that produces carbon dioxide and water.

Laundry Detergent, Glue & Water: Creates slime, also known as oobleck from the Dr. Seuss book Bartholomew and the Oobleck.

Ice Cream & Liquid Nitrogen: Creates ice cream dots sort of like Dippin' Dots ice cream.

Hydrogen Peroxide, Yeast, Water & Dish Soap: This combo creates a foamy fountain that flows out of the container.

Heated Milk & Vinegar: This will create what's called a casein plastic, which can be used to make jewelry and decorations.

Potassium & Water: Potassium is a highly reactive metal and when exposed to water, it will explode.